P9-DHK-741

Hot on Wheels!

The Rally Scene

Written by Jay Denan

Troll Associates

Printed in the United States of America. Troll Associates, Mahwah, N.J.
Library of Congress Catalog Card Number: 79-64701
ISBN 0-89375-258-4 (0-89375-259-2 soft cover ed.)

Photo credits: Jean Rizor, B. McMahon, Fiat, Leyland, Mercedes-Benz, Volvo, Thom Cannell

A sleek Lancia at the Monte Carlo Rally.

It's a trial and a test. It's fun and it's frantic. It's the motor madness that overtakes sports car drivers at certain times during the year. From the logging roads of rural Michigan to the tourist-lined streets of glamorous Monte Carlo, it's the strange racing event known as the *rally*.

Rally cars splash through muddy water...

Is the rally a race? Yes and no. Rallies are not "officially" listed as races. Speed is not the important factor. But time is. However, the rally *does* have a winner, and the course *can* challenge the best of driver, navigator, and machine. Race or trial, challenge or test, the modern rally is an exciting, demanding motor sport that almost anyone can enjoy.

...and speed through rain and fog.

In a rally, racing teams—a driver and a navigator in each car—leave the starting point one minute apart. They race, partly at night, through woods and around hazards. They clack across bridges and groan over deep ruts. They roar across deserts and through snow and ice. Public streets often make up part of the course. Drivers must obey all traffic laws and speed limits.

Approaching a control point.

Along the rally course are *control points.* Each car in a rally is supposed to check into each control point at a stated time. If it doesn't, points are added to the team's score. The lowest score wins a rally.

Rally cars have as many as eight headlights.

What makes a rally truly exciting is that the drivers don't know where they are going! Only the co-driver, or navigator, knows! Navigators are given a route book about five minutes before the race begins. The book lists control points, turns to take, hazards, distances, and time. As the car plunges through the darkness, the navigator snaps out orders to the driver.

A good navigator can feed a driver a lot of information in a very short time. What the navigator says may sound like code —but the driver gets the message. "Go!" the navigator yells to the driver. Then the commands snap out in fast order: "Straight two-tenths. Fast right. T junction, sharp left. Fast! Slight left. Short straight. Right fork. Nearly 90 turn. Now, *now!*"

. . . and into trouble!

Mistakes happen, but a rally team tries to prevent them. For instance, the driver is never supposed to say the word "right." Suppose the navigator calls "Hard left." The driver would answer "Correct." If the driver answered "Right," you can see how confusing it could be! Even so, more than one rally team has suddenly found itself sinking slowly into a bog of mud!

Sometimes they become airborne.

But you don't win a rally on mistakes. It takes hard work and concentration to come in on top. Drivers must know how to handle the car in all situations. Navigators have three big jobs: keep the car on course; give the driver enough information to drive safely and at the correct speeds; and stay on the time schedule.

Navigator and driver must work as a team.

To win a rally, the driver must trust the navigator to call out the right directions. The navigator will lose time by watching the road instead of the map. So, when navigators call out a direction—such as “Hard right”—they don’t look up. They must trust that the driver will not make a “fast left” and spin them smack into a tree! That’s the way to win.

What a rough ride!

Navigators, like drivers, are strapped into their rally cars. But navigators aren't watching the road. So they are whipped around corners and bounced over ruts that they don't see. This rough action often brings on "navigator's illness." They tend to get carsick! So most of them don't eat just before a rally. The rally can be a real endurance test!

Rally fans watch the action at a lonely turn.

People have been testing themselves and their cars at rallies since the beginning of the twentieth century. The first true rally was held in England in 1900. It was called the "1,000 Miles Trial," and it boasted 65 cars. Most of them finished, and the whole thing was so successful that the British have been rally fans ever since.

A high-speed turn on a mountain road.

In 1905, the Herkomer Trial started the kind of rally action that is seen today. The Trial began and ended in Munich, Germany. It included a hillclimb, two speed sections, and a race in one of the city's parks. Out of 89 starting cars, 26 finished without losing a point. The next year the route was made tougher—a longer course, another hillclimb, a mountain run.

Raising dust clouds in an International Rally.

Rallies are now held in many parts of the world, and there are many different kinds. Some are small "scavenger hunt" contests. In these rallies, navigators are kept busy hopping in and out of the car to collect assorted odd items along the way. Some rallies—like Kenya's East African Safari Rally and Britain's Royal Automobile Club Rally—are big names on the sport scene.

Rallies are usually run by automobile clubs. The drivers are usually professionals. The average speed for the rally is limited. Most rallies have special sections where the driver must race against the clock. The winner is decided on the top speed in the special sections, on the timing at the control points, and also on other tests, such as the hillclimb.

Skidding around a turn.

Many rallies are held each year in the United States. Championship events are organized by the North American Rally Racing Association, or NARRA. Prize money and trophies are awarded to the winners. Many local contests are held too. Drivers in these events are usually club members who want to get in on the fun and excitement.

The navigator checks direction and distance.

One of the main problems in staging a rally is where to put it! There are not many usable roads today that can be closed to the public, even for a few hours. And it isn't easy to find an area where cars can race without danger to themselves and others.

Leaving a checkpoint.

A rally, such as the 20 Stages in Grayling, Michigan, might have to get permission from a state department—perhaps the Department of Natural Resources—and the U.S. Forest Service to set up its rally course. Rallies may enlist the help of the local sheriff's office. Deputies may patrol parts of a rally course to keep the public off the roads during the event.

Making up lost time in a cross-continent rally.

The most famous rally is at Monte Carlo, in the tiny European nation of Monaco. When it began in 1911, the Monte Carlo Rally was just a drive to Monaco from different cities in Europe. Later, an 80-kilometer (50-mile) mountain trial was added. Then came a race around Monaco's Grand Prix circuit and a hillclimb. Adding up the winning points began to get very complicated.

Checking the standings.

And, indeed, a rally *is* complicated. In a speed race, it's fairly simple to name the winner—the first car over the finish line. Anyone can *see* that. But a rally needs rules and regulations and time clocks and stopwatches and a lot of paperwork just to find out what has happened, when it's over!

They're off!

Let's join the rally scene backstage to see how it's run. This is an NARRA championship rally, 640 kilometers (400 miles), held on a weekend, in darkness. By Friday night, the teams have arrived. The route books are ready. All the turns, control points, distances, and times are charted and listed. All the cars are ready to go.

What lies ahead?

Just about any car can enter a rally. But to win, it must finish the race. So toughness is more important than top speed. Good headlights, heavy-duty suspension, safe brakes, and the right tires are a must. A car that falls apart every few miles just isn't a rally car—no matter what it cost.

Rugged and reliable.

Then what is a rally car? It is usually heavier and more solid than the small speedsters on the road-racing circuit. Jaguars and Mercedes, Volvos and Fords—and even Jeeps—have all conquered the rally.

Watch that bump!

Whatever the rally car, the racing team carries a lot of equipment inside it. They may need fan belts, gaskets, nuts and bolts, oil, flashlights, a first-aid kit—and even a shovel! Some of the teams carry extra pillows. A long rally can end with a lot of aching bones! Professional rally teams usually wear safety helmets and racing suits.

Splashing through an axle-deep flood.

The driver and the navigator must be ready for anything in a rally. The course may take them along winding forest trails, down steep hills, around hairpin turns, and through axle-deep floods. But they keep going. They want to reach every control point at the right time.

Checking in at a control point.

Since the racing teams must check in at control points, someone must be there to stamp their route cards in and out. That is the job of the *control workers*, who are dropped off at a control point, in the middle of nowhere, in the middle of the night. The workers have a watch, a map, and log sheets.

Extra headlights pierce through the dark.

It seems impossible that any other car will find its way to this deserted spot. But, finally, the miracle happens. Through the trees come the glaring headlights. Another car has made it! Log in and log out. Soon other cars follow in fast order. The quiet control spot isn't quiet or deserted anymore.

The final car is logged out.

When all the cars have been logged in and sent on their way, the control team moves on to a new spot. In a rally of this size, there may be as many as 50 control teams. That may seem like a lot of people scurrying around in the darkness. But the teams know their job. The professional rally is very well organized.

A Porsche roars past observers.

The rally scene has something for everybody. If you're a control worker, you and other "rally freaks" make sure your watches are on time. Your log books are correct. Your control points are covered. When that first car breaks through the darkness, your own special action is coming up!

Approaching a checkpoint at dawn.

If you're the driver, you know your car. You care for it and treat it well. You don't waste time on the course, but you don't abuse that machine either. You can't afford to. It's a long trip and a tiring rally. You both have to last to win.

The winner!

If you're the navigator, you're ready for a long trip too. A long night of T junctions and hard rights and forks to the left. Your head may ache and your stomach jump. But a steady, sure eye on the map and a strong, clear voice will bring you home. It's crazy and wearing and exciting, too. It's your sport—the rally scene.